The Nomad's Trail

Petra Whiteley

Ettrick Forest Press

Ettrick Forest Press

First published 2008
by Ettrick Forest Press
Flat 2f1
109 Corstorphine Road
Edinburgh, EH12 5PZ

www.efpress.com

© Petra Whiteley 2008
Front Cover Image - Katy Jones © 2008
Images 2 & 3 - Sam Ledger © 2008
All other photos - Bartosz Madejski © 2008

All rights reserved. No part of this publication may be reproduced, stored in a retrieval system, or transmitted in any form or by any means, electronic, mechanical, photocopying, recording or otherwise without the prior permission of Ettrick Forest Press.

ISBN : 978 0 9560372 0 6

Layout and Design :
The Copy Bureau Graphics,
3 Exeter Drive, Thornwood
Partick, Glasgow, G11 7UY.
Tel : 0141 337 3419

Printed and bound by :
Clydeside Press Ltd, 37 High Street,
Glasgow, G1 1LX.

Contents

1. Revelations
2. These pages
3. Petals of life
4. Scent of tomorrows
5. Sunday afternoon
6. The twinning
7. Neverland is her oyster
8. Stories of travelling
10. The late night train
11. Black birds and white cars
12. Clouds
13. River singing
14. At the gates
15. Broken plumbing
16. A day of a dog's life
17. Duets
18. Nomad's trail
21. I don't write poetry today
23. The scales
24. This wasn't our first kiss
25. Spring violins
26. Moonchild
28. Dissolving
29. Rising hope
31. Why?
33. Word birds
34. Alchemy of burning angels
35. Just as we are
37. Train tracks
38. Incantation for Eve

Petra Whiteley was born in the Czech Republic.
She studied Economics, Czech, English and Literature.

She immigrated to England in 1993 and has worked in a
variety of jobs. She lives in North Dorset with her young
daughter and plans to move to Essex in 2009
to live with her partner.

She is passionate about poetry, literature,
art, science and music.

Acknowledgements

My heartfelt thanks go to -

Katherine and Sarah Whiteley, Richard Cox and Sarah Porter who had stood by my side for the last decade and their love and support had always been the light in hard times and to many others who made my life richer for knowing them.

To Graham Hardie who had shown great faith in my work and given me support and made this possible.

To Daniel Miles for his love, steadfast loyalty, his open heart and inspiration; for standing by my side, holding my hand in the rain and for encouraging me to live my dreams.

To Dale Winslow and Connie Stadler for priceless advice and encouragement, saying the right words at the right time, inspiration and friendship.

To Samantha Ledger and Bartosz Madejski for allowing me to have their art in some of these pages, thanks go to Sam for encouragement too.

And also to Craig Podmore, Will Marshe, Frank Axworthy, Larry Kuechlin, Charles Leogrande, Gina, Nicole… and many others who had supported my work with warm words of encouragement and interest.

Dedicated to my daughter and to my poet.

Revelations

I'm the blue rug-cloth wrung out hard
by strong grip of many maudlin hands,
my core is dried out, known - thus forgotten.

My heart's likeness rests in red sparrows' beaks
eaten, hollowed out to fragile bone marrow:
sacrificed on an altar for sharp stare of vermilion God.

My soul is burdened by opaque, hard etched stones
buried in the mud of sullen wild rivers' thirst,
it cannot rise only hear the sound of hooves of black horse.

In barren fields northern winds blow dark ribbon of fate forth
and back with relentless rhythm, rage-tied beat in dry bracken -
its slow hissing extinguishes smouldering embers of silent ambition.

Truth falls into black holes of other world's lies, specks
of spider-web veins drawn into the wrinkles of grievous longing.
Fingers shape vases of wonders and dreams that are broken in the kiln.

Starlight, I won't taste you, hold you tight in my shaking arms.
All I ever wanted was to hold on. My life ignited in your promises
of never fading away; never slipping away, and now I have revelations.

Revelations of grey distorted mirrors of abandonment in translucent flesh,
oracle breaths carry ruby shards on bloodied memories of nearly dying,
I will live when spellbound lilac fairy children come to nest in my womb
again.

On my knees I silently whisper your many names, your many faces,
my hair swept away and flowing behind, on corroding cliffs I stand,
wondering where all this has begun, left shivering for a sense of freedom.

These pages

You love pages of your books virginally white,
their new smell captured in flickering tempo of clock.
It reminds me of the way you read me like a novel
my gestures and silences, even my odd pages,
complicated stresses and foreign punctuation marks.

I love my books showing their history, their life,
looking inhabited and comfortable, as in a librarian's home,
I absorb words out of them, cover my sleep in a sentence.

We'd love to wipe the sorrows from marking the print,
write our dreams in not too neat writing in note chapters.

Days are spent in pursuit of the fickle taunting Muses.
You're near me and my blood feels a change, swirling
inside veins of your seraphic stanzas, and a sonata
for a good verse is written in beauty of Helicon springs.
I wonder if we could free fall through time's helix.

You'd have been a troubadour with such clean notes rising,
and beautiful stories falling from your full lips and smile.
I'd dance to your words in perfected pirouettes and dream.
We'd collect coins in the cities, from streets of Paris,
Vienna to hustle of London, in the hues of so many colours.

Carry this history to keep dear in the greyness of modern cultures,
where language has died and is dissected on post mortem table,
stinking of formaldehyde and sterilised sharp instrumentation,
germ free and stripped bare naked, hairless, gathered around
desolation, confessions of cruel cold times, and pure madness.

photo by Bartoz Madejski

Petals of life

Recesses of darkness,
shelter of silken hoping,
grasp loose in mid-way.

I smelt the blood red
sea of roses,
petals of life
embracing gentleness of winds -
the slow breath of God,
it lingered
and lured me -
into wanting, reaching,
needing.

I was standing behind
the barbed wire
and the green-mossed
hands of royal lions,
contorted faces and gargoyles,
Entwined in bouquets of flowers.

The red and purple
filling translucent skin,
the metallic taste
of blood covering lips
that let go of innocence,
whispering words
to disappear into,
then the small hands
folding the world
into torn pockets.

Blood red roses -
they were inside me,
but they were not to be mine.

For me, procession
of fears paraded
to precision of drums.

photo by Sam Ledger

Scent of tomorrows

Smell of summer grass,
the heart of sacredness
lingers with mist and dew
on vivid film of memories.

Sometimes it's hard to play
them all back for longing
swells oceans, swallows
resolve to resist desire
to dissolve into the oceans
and be carried into purity
of never-being, never holding
onto a body, a breath.

But for those times
I am captured, I hold onto
those fine moments
in your arms, and after
when you still gaze into
my eyes and your happiness
twirls and blends
with colours of mine.

Before I knew you,
I buried my heart
under the linden tree,
ashen burnt, wounded,
I walked like a stranger,
and painted expressions
on unchangeable numbness.

Sorrow-tied, I held your
hand and let go,
burst into the skies
and found myself looking
forward countless tomorrows
in the glow of your passionate eyes.

Sunday afternoon

I simmer Sunday afternoon
in punk music, loud
with smell of full English,
whiff of unwashed dishes.

Trying to caffeinate the time
into the unwilling Mondays,
looking into divining the fate
of declining Sun to fill in
that everyone I love
lives too far.

Today loneliness
tastes of stale tea,
broken biscuits
and dried leaves
gathering to perish
the long nights.

The twinning

I bend luminous essence of your exhales
  into the painted glass of our even windows.

        The twinned sister is a multiplication
        of cut-paper silhouettes on white walls.

The guillotine is her voice, she knows
  the sentence, it is the rattles and clicks

        of fairy-tale dragon-mouth, which yields scruples
        with the handful of ashes. The muddy sacrifice

at the hammered feet of arrow-shaped giants, as
  they bark orders for paying the piggy-eyed price -

        for rejection from the inhale - the silent womb
        of life, the crushing crime of birth into cold.

The unending war of human beings against nature,
  the neurotic spillage of blood and crushed heads.

        The muted enclave does not hold hands, covered in
        marked words, with stabs in their silken-rough backs.

But the hands come together to pat the adopted
  daughter on colourless hair, and together, they

        feed the diaphanous strangeness of her. As she
        starts bending words into ribbons of her boat.

Watch her go where she will not have to

        whisper.

Neverland is her oyster

(for Jessie)

*I held you all night
of your reluctant birth,
you were supposed
to be hazy of sight,
but your eyes firmly
focused on mine,
and everything that
could ever be said,
passed between
your gaze
and my tracing
of your perfection.*

Today,
you sing Christmas carols
in the eve of summer,
you run and skip,
spread your arms wide,
because you are
Peter Pan
and Neverland
is your oyster.

And I hope that you will
never let them tell you,
that girls can't be
just like
Peter Pan,
and that girls
cannot fly.

Because you can

and you do...so high!

Stories of travelling

Light ivory mist hangs on meadows, half-clothed oaks -
like a lover tenderly pressing kisses on velvet-soft skin.
Sheep grazing, strewn like dusty diamonds over resting
fields. The turn of wheels, train cutting the landscape
like a sturdy knife cuts through layers of birthday cake -
icing: slowness of morning movements, softened tones.

Inside a lone traveller
darkest red raindrops fall,
they slither on trembling
scraped flesh, saddened lips.

City clutching blanket of bitter midnight, fluorescent lights glisten
with stolen glow of Evenstar, wet pavements adorned with cracked
jewels of blemished century - Mecca of rubbish, discarded people
blending with the languid night-trickling crowds , rushing blind,
missing souls that float just under the black swollen clouds, heavy
eyes of brooding skies seek the tones of harpsichord, still playing.

A lone figure strokes
passionate notes, singing
hallelujah. Maybe the rain
falling - are Lord's tears?

Night's in smithereens, morning tide brings light, coffee aromas are
seeping out of cafeterias; shy sun warms up exposed skin un-noticed.
Trains are pulling out of stations and suited strangers' talk in coded
language, clutching morning papers. I sit by the steamed doors, stifled
life escapes from my dust filled lungs, questions die on my tongue,
vapours - new-born dreams envelop my sorrow-sloven heart -
you kissed me as I lay still.

Along the bridge I walk
into the smile that keeps
me warm, eyes ablaze,
breathing in the air of change.

And if we will have to scatter the ashes of our lavish dreams -
will you always remember me? Or will you smother the memories
down into dungeons of your mind? Will you tear spring blooms
from stems and throw them in the wintry gales and move so fast,
that the skeletons of vagrant visions under Juniper trees will
shake and fall apart into oblivion's kiss with our names broken?

The subject tonight...
is learning how to keep
our eyes open.

In the hum of the steel machines
a woman in yellow dress waves
at every passing cloud, she
stands quietly in the field
with the nostalgic lilac smells
washing over her tired feet.

We never see her, just like we
never see a speck of dust,
and just like the dirt,
we keep missing her,
she, the inner beat
of life.

The late night train

We slipped through the darkness,
amongst the screams and songs of drunks;
you and I, my hands high on hold of yours,
my soul soaked with your heart.

Redemption crept from your eyes,
and I found myself freed from my muteness,
telling you things I hid from myself too.

Yesterday, I looked for the storm
that used to circle my heart
as familiar as my disgust
married to my guilt,
and I saw it left me
through some sliding door.

Today, I found keeping a promise -
a certain possibility as it all
sunk in.

Black birds and white cars

Just imagine a black bird
driving a white car.

Not just that, the black bird
wearing a police uniform
and the siren blasting
and deafening the town.

Will the man next-door stop arguing
and smackin' the left ear of his son
and let his tantrum go?
Will the Jehovah witness
stop knocking on my door
telling me I'm damned
and He can save my soul?

And would that black bird
leave the white car
in the street and come in
for a quick cup of tea...

And will half of my street
not steal the car for a fix?
And will the other not gossip
for a month and a half?

Clouds

On Friday morning,
I left the house in heaven.
I've collected the clouds
put them into the machine
programmed: on delicates
originally, at least.
I thought I'd give them what for,
turned up the temperature,
and gave it the best soap.

Nobody thanked me
for sunny day henceforth,
or praised my benevolent mind,
but oh well, I knew all this:
you people, are ungrateful lot
and me, a very upset God;

from now on:
rain and thunder!

River singing

Come closer,
my quiet lover,
with summer
scented letters,
ever so softly sent
where snow flowers
with bluebells,

 where the night
is never long enough...

And then,
in the sliced time
of daydreaming hands
of river singing time,

we will wait and whisper
tender incantations
to become the slivers
of light on the waves
chasing the reflections
of naked moon and stars.

At the gates

The skies are emptied into the shadows
of these hard steeled walls.

Chains are dripping silent morning rain
covered in a film of sticky oil.

The swords are melted with delirious
lips of malicious gargoyles and reach out high.

These gothic symbols
are not a map to salvation.

They twist in the dark - lead to the touch
of crooked hands of God's torn self.

I am my own eye of the wailing tempest.
It consumes the rivers of my anaemic blood.

Thirst settles and holds on to drained skin.
Exhausted muscles harden into boulders of granite.

Knuckles bleed in ominous patterns that mesmerise
mind's searching tentacles into recesses of mouldy rancour.

Grave sunk in reluctant light of dawn hides past in golden
letters and wilted flowers; grief pierces frozen ashes, stirs shadows.

Bury me in this dark soil and sing those songs to me, I will await
the rebirth in innocence from memories of drowning and suffocation.

I will lie in the embrace of the only loving ancestors and dream
of your touch. The night of the soul will be faced with steady glaze.

I will resurrect my fallen soul in a theatre of so many shades of reds,
of dusks upon the green hills adorned with white horses of hope.

photo by Sam Ledger

Broken plumbing

Molly, who lived on the third floor
always wore pigtails and spend time
turning Shakespeare's tragedies
into scripts of porn.

That terrible day, whilst her mind had
gone to explore the possibilities,
she heard noises,

dog scratching the door,
she brushed it aside.
few hours later:
bang! The high ceiling
of the fourth level came down.

Broken plumbing should never
be ignored!

A day of a dog's life

My owner is a bastard:
never gives me food to eat!
Scavenge I must.
Hide I must
or else into the cage
I will be confined
and howl the loss
of my freedom to move.
That damn freedom of barking
will be good for nothing:
nobody will hear me...
I'm the oppressed class
of the animals under the yoke
of the ruling class
of so called humans.
So don't ever ask me again
how the dog's day like mine
went ticking away
or else I'll bite your arse.

Duets

(for Dan)

We sail pure white sheets
of awakened
nakedness -
florid weir of ardour's
honey of summer storms.

    You paint
contours of my landscape,
curving
in smudges of charcoal
and moon's pallor,
bathed in russet and indigo.

    I paint
your smooth coffeed skin
in sun-touched waves
of sea's cerulean and
letters in ink of red hair.

In my depths,
you find my lost, forgotten voice
and melt yours
            within,
                      without.

Fire light flickers
in symphony
to a duet of hearts in one beat.

This metamorphosis
of rhythms blending
new colours,

exhaling,
exulting,

blissfully nailed
to the tangle of our bodies.

Nomad's trail

In this town
Death runs the council
and I form
and give shy smiles
to work-walking strangers,
just to feel
that I could fill
this shivering body
with presence
within heartbeat,
still after all these
unbelonging years.

Sometimes
I hurt for deepest red
to fill the sky
and fall on
my lips in the rain
as it migrates
from my slow
flowing blood
into the laughter
of the perfected
condescendence
of breaking angels.

I've always been
a nomad and now,
every morning
my burning skin
of trembling fingers
traces my mortality
in the cracks of walls,
longing for the spirals
to become one with
the feverish heart -
I've heard inside the soil
and blackberry blossoms.

Bliss of lost clouds
amongst dancing stars...

With the turn
of Earth's body
I hear the night calls,
the trees touching,
whispering, beckoning,
the creatures of night,
confidently inhabiting
the spaces between,
their freedom crawls
inside my breath, still
trapped to the vibration
of sound frequencies
filled by the prism of light,
nailing me down
into the settler's way.

The life I have:
mimicry.

Unconceivable.

In lonely streets
I whisper to those taken
by north western winds,
the ruby glass shatters
and pricks my soul.

The lost traveller's blood,
cries in timbers of summer,
begs to be poured out,
fly with the grace of cranes.

Sometimes, it just is a time -
a time to go...

I don't write poetry today

It writes Mucha on round table,
thin shadows of fake flowers
on cappuccino walls.

Homemade scones glazed
by child's excitement
of culinary grail
from her own fingers.

Scattered pieces of drawings,
treasure maps to never-lost
childhood days, lines
of toys with secret lives.

Silver heart and
football mementoes,
reflections of a lover,
invoked in pining hours.

I don't write poetry today.

It writes scribbles on
cooling glimmers of light,
estranged by movement -
left stroking last fruits,
now too ripe
and nearly rotting.

Golden bushes shaking
in wind gaining on rage,
drying leaves crumbling
under rushing feet.

I don't write poetry today.

It writes the air
that already smells of
Halloween, dark streets
and broken lamps
with drizzle seeping
into sun-grieving skin.

The passing trains
with time lost in landscapes
that call memento mori,
strangers smile more urgently -
'remember that I've been
a human being, not an automata
of this strange century.'

I don't write poetry today

It writes the books
on shelves unread
and waiting for pages
to be turned and scenes
acted in imagination.

I don't write these words,
they write me.

I stood in front of a fence
all day, they wouldn't come in.

So instead
I hide on tomorrow's
unwritten pages,
promising
I'll catch those words
and live through
the myriad of colours
of their wings.

The scales

When I saw her in town after
quite a long time, I asked her
about how's she's been
and what's she's been up to.

She said
how much she hates being asked
what she does for a living,
as if her job defined
her as a human being.

When she came for a cup of tea
she told me about how she lost
a ring in Somerfield, how she
asked a shop assistant and they
found it together.

So I said, do you mean
the kind lady called Sue,
whose daughter of eighteen
works in there too?

She did answer, but still ...
she didn't get my drift.

Although it was not as
head-shaking a moment as
reading Nietzsche and
his Übermensch concept,

I thought it rather
strange that we live in
the same world, but at the
same time on a different planet.

photo by Bartoz Madejski

This wasn't our first kiss

Dusk shadows of forests deepen;
pearls on the azure are covered
under the blanket of indigo to black haze.
We see the first stars shine in stirring cold,
we point and give them our names.
We wage rebellion on night-abandoned
perfection of golf-course grass.
Drunk, and drunk with touch of dust
of enchantment of falling in love.

This bond, this only sacredness
I hold close to my heart.
This bliss without words
in which all life of the soul
in love disappears;
how the sky bends across
with such purity
and all the earth's strife
becomes so alien to us!
And how the night shines
in splendour of memory's crown!

Spring violins

God, I beseech you to render
the fast life-shapes of clouds to me,

I will pull their milk-tender
softness through my mind,

forget discordant moments unseen
in changing eyes, because my dreams ...

they're still the same, foreseen,
hidden in trees with baby leaves,

passing by windows. We are reborn
to weak spring Sun. We cried nightly

to the forever grey of winters,
now we breathe freedom, defined

by warmth melting the clinging
remains of dark biting deer hearts

of inner-living landscapes deeply.
And where this slow smile begins,

we will dance to lilac violins
to the rhythm of morning soul.

Living,

passionate steps...

of the dance.

Moonchild

Moonchild,

First sign of preciousness . . .

Sacrificed on alabaster altars
Eyes piercing through centuries
Of dreaming.
You belong to soft whispers
of summer solstice flowers,
adorning the hair of Branwen.

Moonchild,

Take me to you now!

Moonchild,

Wave your dreams
through silver hair
of the stormy winds
of my inner world.

I want to reach
. . . Now . . . .
. . . . . .Now . . .
I want the sign of preciousness

the pull of tides
the pull of Moonchild

He calls me from the depths;
my soul disappears
into moonstone yearning.

In landscape frozen in silence
I was still and unfulfilled.

Moonchild,

sound the bells
and treasured songs
from ancestral South.

Moonchild,

I long to hear the wings
of angels migrating
to warmer shores
of my awoken being.

It is my uncried tears they seek

Arisen around the break
Of the misty dawn
He is beautiful
Withdrawn
Powerful
Distant
Brave
Depressive
Amazing
Forever never good enough.

photo by Bartoz Madejski

Dissolving

Smoke of premonitions crawls
through my soul, sown from mute fire,
glowing embers - the keepsakes.

I open the windows,
and they disappear in the morning air.

And I long...
to just be... just float on myriad of
tingling words, sun-like, dunk in waves
of soothing arms of colossal statues,
perfumed by maternal breath of life.

Embraced,
        clear.
Slate wiped clean.

Dissolving,
in flowing robes of the angel
of ancient light of eyes,
their gift of forgetfulness
and flying high, resting
in the soft of my palms.

Rising Hope

I lay my face down
Where eyes never fall
inside the sharp elbow
of the Green man's creek
clutching on soiled reeds
covered in nightmares.

I can't stop;
I swallow and define
the minute's rise and fall,
by the shadows
the sun throws on grass
and hide,
for the Priest of thorns
is coming to collect the tithe
of pain and doubts.

The rhythm of the horse hooves;
an elegant march of fears
revealed in the slivered light
of shaking trees
and the beat of following wings:
a sky covered in the hunger
of deathly birds.

I slip into the river
holding fast
the carnelian snowflakes
you left behind in footprints
to seek the look of your eyes
in the ruins
of rising hope.

Where the bluebells
shelter the fallen
I come back to free
my gypsy heart.
And here, you and I,
dance to the thunder
and lightning held
in the creases of your palms.

Why?

Why did you hit the ground three times?

I hold your breath tucked inside my palms
as freezing, silent nights loyally guard
their diamond whispers with black moon

Why did you leave in disguise of morning clouds?

I've seen you standing in the eye of the furious winds
hair flowing; hands strong;
holding on to the haunting spectre of time

Why does the cello stop in a third of forgotten concertos?

Your movements; elegant and mesmerising:
the poisoned waves of wrathful ocean
keeping our history of love under brooding tides

Why is the broken sky crying?

Moonlight is troubling my memory.
I scratch at walls of smoky air
screaming the secret name of your soul

Why are the fires absorbing hopes?

Hearts fragile, so impossible to break
as it's always been....this look of tragedy
in a ceaseless sound of migrating wings

Why are mute angels seeking the cradle of passion?

I thought I'd loose you when darkness fell
you've changed it all for me, and I,
resolved, touch the dawn of abandonment

Why is the devil living inside deep red blood?

If I could, I would bring the azure blankets
of soothing tomorrows, instead of searching
inside these empty Celtic vases of fallen roses

Why is the silence reaching the path of wilderness?

This fluorescence inside your words of forgiveness...
the light that stays in the midst of these fields of filth
I clutch inside, my fists bleeding against the savage storms

Why have we forgotten how to dance flamenco?

These longing woods, I've embraced for more than thousand days,
whisper the contents of my heart to waiting soil
for French daffodils of immortal love

Why is my heart spinning in singing heartbeats?

Is this what would be if we'd truly seen the encrypted rocks;
before we forgot the shivers running down our spines
resonating with the rapid fall from Universe to forsaken Earth?

Word birds

Word birds with feathers of Zen
flew in countless patterns
on a page of my dreaming mind.

Awoken by blunted morning light,
I begin to search creases in memory
for softness of the song they sung.

Perhaps,
        in
              vain.

Alchemy of burning angels

Burning angels
Standing in a long queue
Their alabaster faces turned
Ever so slightly, ever so gracefully
Reading the sky, never standing still
The blue and white pierced by cries
Of red, dark as revenge of the storm

In the silence, I feel this coming over
And I am too, about to
shiver and turn away

I still feel you
Watching me.

photo by Bartoz Madejski

Just as we are

Supposing that our hearts are
laid on the table, still pulsing
with poker faces of everyday living
mixed with undertow of what is real.

Imagine white lace cloth, with tea
spoons smudged with rust of history
will be our silver haired judge
and bloodshot-eyed jury of twelve.

They will be washed in saline water
from midnight black of whispering
oceans; they will measure carefully
the units of what we've been through.

Will we be watching the heavy doors
just to hear wisdom on the instep
of the absent-minded God, or watch the
windows in case he flies like angels?

But suppose that this riddle needs not
be weighted down by beauty of dreams
of swan-like Icaruses, or to be made
shining with golden love of Prometheus

and his line of martyrs. Will we not
remember that we slept under the same
linen, same stars? Is holding hands not
worthy of highest perception of beauty?

And why must we be laughed at from dark
corners as if we were less than living?
For being just like this, feet sinking
into moist earth that has no secrets,

that for us the movement of wind in trees
is bereft of portent and will of Sun, and
relics fallen from effervescent Moon legends
are just bed time stories and anecdotes.

Supposing our hearts are not flattened
by this lack, can we be silent and yet
singing, humming the soothing notes, just
as we are, for a bit longer, and our sound

hollow the judgements from the broken horns?

And rest, just for this while, and here, just
as we are, beyond the mirage of Elysian fields.

photo by Bartoz Madejski

Train tracks

Dirtied silver beams
of train tracks
thread my veins and arteries
into the curling paths
of horizons that lay
between us.

I approach
cracks of pavements
where we stumbled
in larking abandon,
as I see the tattered
Christmas tree
in pub window,
it begins to choke me
on rose scented nostalgia.

Heartbeat of whispers
inside folds of memories -
solar jewels
strewn on the fabric
of gossamer days,
sunk in longing
and waiting.

For the way
your eyes hold me,
and for the view
of the world
from the warmth
of your strong arms.

I'll never be
any good at writing
any kind of a love poem,
my love for you
patiently lies beyond
any words that can ever
be written or said.

Incantation for Eve

I am
    pretty
        practical
myth.
    An incarnation
of functional helpfulness,

            So many uses for....

My heart - quartered on the chopping board,
        many fine knives blunted...

My mind - portioned into tidy compartments, covered
        in foil in fridge-freezer, long-lasting.

My soul - cleansed with the dishes and silverware:
        of dirt of life, of soiled veins, stained gender.

    In the night, I am
fragmented into a thousand shards,
glued together by the sense of the edge, the disturbance
            of tepid waves -
stagnant lakes....this modern theatre of monologues -
murmuring madness inside grey walls.

    I must... paint.. myself...
in brightest reds, measure the cells carefully,
           perfectly
and as it
    should
        be....
dictated...in hyped verse.

Clapping on signal... applaud this empty void
              of needy designs, manic make-believe masks.

Who am I?
              That which I steal from mournful rows of
morning crows - their hollow shrieks.
And after, when used and devoid of meaning,
   search for another state of being - by you,
                                          by me....

It has begun - invention of rose without thorns,
              without wilting,
The holy grail.
              But what is it?

Whatever it is, it is an omen of my failure,
abstracted valuation, and commoditisation.
Dismemberment of the string of love,
to be recycled, re-used. An item
of second-hand market, then landfill.

What are the names of my sin?

The sin of birth,
         sin of giving,
                  of bleeding,
of giving birth,
                  mystery of languid
fading out
         into the Unknown.

And I will fill the casts of lighter
                            graceful smiles.

photo by Bartoz Madejski